Catheri

Shang-a-Lang

faber and faber

First published in 1998
by Faber and Faber Limited
3 Queen Square, London WC1N 3AU

Typeset by Country Setting, Kingsdown, Kent CT14 8ES
Printed in England by Intype London Ltd

© Catherine Johnson, 1998

Catherine Johnson is hereby identified as author
of this work in accordance with Section 77 of the
Copyright, Designs and Patents Act 1988

A CIP record for this book
is available from the British Library

ISBN 0-571-20077-X

2 4 6 8 10 9 7 5 3 1

Characters

The Girls' Chalet

Jackie
Lauren
Pauline

The Boys' Chalet

Vince
Carl

For Gina Maeleka
1958-1995

Shang-a-Lang opened at the Bush Theatre, London, on 11 November 1998. The cast was as follows:

Carl Stephen Graham
Vince Peter Jonfield
Lauren Ona McCracken
Jackie Joanne Pearce
Pauline Nicola Redmond

Directed by Mike Bradwell
Designed by Geoff Rose
Lighting by Chahine Yavroyan
Sound by Mic Pool

Act One

Somerwest World – Butlins, Minehead '98. November.
As the lights go down, we hear a loud siren – the
opening to 'Blockbuster', by The Sweet. Spotlight on
Pauline, Jackie and Lauren, standing close together, by
a microphone. They're wearing clothes and platform
shoes, looking happy but a bit nervous – they're about
to give it a bit of karaoke. The music begins – just the
backing track. As they sing, they appear to be following
the words on an unseen screen.

Jackie/Lauren
Aa – aaa.

Pauline
You'd better beware, you'd better take care,
You'd better watch out if you've got long black hair.
He'll come from behind – you'll go out of your mind.
You'd better not go, you never know what you'll find.

Jackie/Lauren
Aa – aaa.

Pauline You'll look in his eyes – don't be surprised
If you don't know what's going on behind his disguise.
Nobody knows – Blockbuster goes,
He'll steal your woman out from under your nose.

Jackie
Does anyone know the way? Did we hear someone say?

Lauren (*pouting*)
We just haven't got a clue what to do –

Jackie
Does anyone know the way? There's got to be a way –

Pauline/Jackie/Lauren To BLOCKBUSTER!

*Lights down. The music continues, on a cassette
player – this time the Sweet version.*
Lights up on:

SCENE ONE

Girls' Chalet.
*There are two single beds, with flowery duvets; a
white, plastic table with two white plastic chairs; a
wash-basin with a large mirror. There is a door leading
to the bathroom and front-door.*
*The girls' cassette recorder is on the table, playing a
70s compilation tape. Also on the table; two white
pyrex cups and saucers, and a little white box with
complimentary tea bags and coffee sachets. There's a
jumble of make-up, shampoo and hair spray on the
wash-basin stand, and an opened bottle of vodka and a
can of Red Bull.*
*Pauline, wearing her 'glam' and platforms, is perched
on the edge of her bed, reading her 'Festival of the 70s'
brochure, and sipping a vodka and Red Bull in a
tumbler. There's a pile of clothes on the bed, all 70s
stuff. Pauline's singing along to the track as she reads:*

Pauline . . . the cops are out, they're running about . . .
(*Calls toward door.*) . . . hey, Jac – they've got a
Mongolian barbecue, what's that, stir fried yak? . . .

No reply – she isn't really expecting one.

. . . fucking hell, breakfast's at nine – that's a joke, innit?

Jackie comes through from the bathroom, wearing the same clothes as in the Prologue, but topped with a 'glam' wig. It's the first time she's worn these clothes, and she's not sure about them. Pauline gives her a whistle.

Jackie Do I look all right?

Pauline Gob-smacking.

Jackie totters over to the mirror, to check, Pauline returns to her brochure.

Pauline . . . 'there is always fish as an alternative to breakfast' . . . Fuck that, I'm having me fry-up . . .

Jackie (*turns*) We haven't got to have cooked breakfast, have we?

Pauline Too right, it's paid for.

Jackie But I never eat breakfast, it's how I keep my weight down.

Pauline Leave off, Jac, you don't need to diet. You look great.

Jackie For my age.

Pauline Yeah, well, neither of us is going to pass for twenty again, thirty neither, come to that . . .

Jackie . . . speak for yourself.

She turns back to the mirror, looks at herself, and snatches off the wig.

I can't go out like this!

Pauline 'Course you can –it's a 70s weekend, everyone's going to be dressed up. You saw those blokes in reception, done out like The Glitter Band.

Jackie Yeah, but it's alright when you're team-handed, looks a bit silly just the two of us.

Pauline I don't think so. I think it looks good we've made an effort. (*Beat.*) D'you reckon I should've invited more people?

Jackie You did, didn't you?

Pauline Yeah, but we sort've knew Lauren'd never get her arse in gear to get down here . . . I only asked her 'cos I felt sorry for her.

Jackie Lauren? Why?

Pauline I don't know – sometimes, when I'm behind the bar, I see her sitting with all the cider heads, and I think, what she used to be like, she was so pretty . . .

Jackie . . . everyone fancied her.

Pauline Everyone fucked her.

They both laugh. Pauline gets up and pours more vodka in her glass.

Pauline Jac?

Jackie No, ta. (*She tries the wig on again.*) . . . oh, I don't know . . . what else've you got?

As Jackie starts to go through Pauline's clothes again, Pauline sits back down and picks up the brochure.

Pauline . . . right, eight o'clock, Oasis Bar, it's Maggie May – hem, Rod Stewart tribute band . . .

Jackie . . . this stuff is brilliant, Pauline, where d'you get it all?

Pauline . . . oh, charity shops, some of it's mine . . . *But.* Eight o'clock in the Mirage Bar, it's the Sensational Soul Brothers, with their covers of the classic 70s soul-trax . . .

Jackie . . . oh, them, definitely – I love soul . . .

Pauline . . . yeah, and the Rod Stewart band's female – that's a bit wank . . . so, at nine forty-five . . .

Jackie (*over her, holding up a sparkly green halter neck*) Ooh, I used to have one like this . . .

Pauline (*under*) . . . over at The Oasis, it's Rosetta Stone, what the fuck did they do . . . ?

Jackie (*continued*) . . . hang on – this *is* mine, you thieving cow . . .

Pauline . . . it's not . . .

Jackie . . . it bloody *is* – I remember – you borrowed it for the school disco. That night you knocked off with Nicky Evans.

Pauline I never knocked off with Nicky Evans! He's got no arms.

Jackie He still got his hands up that halter – neck. You told me. (*teasing*) Nick Thalid. You could really pull in those days, Paul . . .

Pauline Ha-ha.

Jackie You do remember, don't you?

Pauline No, I was drunk.

Jackie Oh God, me too – wasn't that the night you, me and Lauren were drinking cider and black, and she passed out on the playground? Mr Owen had to take her home in his car.

Pauline Oh yeah. Here, I bet he didn't take her *straight* home.

Jackie Didn't she tell you?

Pauline's look says she didn't.

Oh well, I guess she didn't really want it getting around. They were having a right old ding-dong those two.

Pauline . . . I knew that . . .

Jackie Lauren said they did it in the lay-by. Well, he did, she was still paralytic . . . (*She laughs.*) . . . he'd never get away with it now . . .

Pauline No, that's child abuse, and rape, now.

Jackie Yeah. S'pose it is. Still, we had a laugh, didn't we? Young, free and single.

Pauline I'm *still* young, free and single.

Jackie Oh, not for much longer, Paul.

Pauline Thanks very much!

Jackie I wasn't on about your age! That comes later . . . no, I just meant, you'll meet someone. I know you will . . .

Pauline Nicky Evans is married. She's quite nice . . .

Jackie You don't want Nicky Evans, do you?

Pauline No. Just *he* can do it . . .

Jackie . . . and so can you. Don't you meet blokes in the bar?

Pauline The only handsome strangers in my life are brewery reps. And they're all fucking nauses.

Jackie They're not!

Pauline Yes, they are. They're right creeps. That's why they're reps.

Jackie (*unsure*) But how d you know?

Pauline Know what?

Jackie That they're all fucking horses?

Pauline 'Nauses' – you dollop! I said they're all 'nauses'.

She waggles her little finger at Jackie. They are both laughing.

. . . couldn't fuck a rat, that lot . . .

Jackie . . . oh God, I don't believe it . . . ! I really thought you said . . . oh, I haven't laughed like this in ages . . .

Pauline (*sings Carpenters*)
'We've only just begun . . . '

Jackie (*sings*)
. . . to live . . .

Pauline (*sings*)
'White lace and promises – a kiss for luck and we're on our way . . . '

Jackie You've got weddings on the brain!

Pauline Have not.

Jackie I know why. Mr Right is just around the corner – you can feel it in your bones . . .

Pauline Yeah, yeah . . .

Jackie . . . that's why we're here. It's Fate. Tonight, you'll meet the man of your dreams.

Pauline And lie about my age.

Jackie You don't, do you?

Pauline Thirty-five.

Jackie Blimey. Don't you worry people might think you look a bit . . . ?

Pauline . . . rough?

Jackie No! – Just, you don't look thirty-five, Paul . . .

Pauline Tough. 'Cos I am. I'm telling you now, it's what men want – 24 to 35, you look in the ads . . . us mature girls have had it.

Jackie Blimey. I'd better start lopping off a couple of years, then.

Pauline Why? You're not looking for another man, are you?

Jackie No . . .

There's a knock at the door, emphatic, several times. Both women jump.

Who's that?

Pauline I don't know. Perhaps it's your Rob, he's changed his mind and you got to go home.

Jackie (*this is a possibility*) Don't be daft . . .

Pauline (*getting up*) . . . or maybe it's my mystery man, come to whisk me away from all this . . .

Jackie . . . can't be Nicky, with a knock like that.

Pauline Who says he's using his hand?

She exits, as Jackie says 'ugh'. When Pauline is off, Jackie checks her watch. It's getting on, she needs to make a call. She finds her bag under the clothes pile and looks for her purse. Meanwhile, off, we hear Pauline open the door and hear the following exchange –

Lauren (*off*) Aagh!

Pauline (*off*) Oh, my God!

Lauren (*off – laughing*) You look menkle!

Jackie's turning, not looking pleased. Lauren comes into the room, holding a carrier bag. She's got long, blonde hair, quite matted, and is wearing a long, black skirt, a black mohair jumper, motor-cycle boots. She's got masses of silver bangles on her arm and her nose is pierced. She laughs again and points at Jackie.

Lauren Fuckin 'ell! . . .

Pauline's coming in behind Lauren, shaking her head at Jackie, behind Lauren's back.

. . . this is like a time warp, or summat! I gotta get changed . . .

She puts her carrier bag on the other bed.

Is this mine?

Jackie No, it's mine . . .

Pauline (*at the same time*) . . . Lauren, what are you doing here?

Lauren Shut up, you know why I'm here. You asked me.

Lauren takes a bottle of cider from her carrier.

Lauren Brought a bottle.

Pauline Yeah, but the last time I spoke to you, you said you were really skint and you hadn't booked . . .

Lauren's gone over to the table, to open the cider and pour some into a cup.

Pauline . . . I thought you weren't coming.

Lauren I know – isn't it brilliant!

She raises her cup

Cheers! (*spots something*) Ooh, vodka . . .

Lauren heads for the vodka bottle to mix with the cider. Jackie's just watching her, guardedly.

13

Pauline Yeah, but how did you get here? And how d'you find the chalet?

Lauren Well . . . (*She sips the vodka and cider.*) . . . mmm lush . . . last night, Tony Clarke came round, and I was telling him I was really pissed off I couldn't come away with you two, so he said he'd give me a lift down.

Pauline What for?

Lauren What do you mean – what for?

Pauline I know Tony Clarke. Never summat for nothing.

Lauren (*vaguely*) I don't know . . . p'raps he likes me . . .

Pauline gives Jackie a look.

Lauren . . . anyway I asked at reception where you was, and when they got distracted by some blokes doin' mooners, I sneaked in.

Jackie I knew it.

Pauline Lauren!

Lauren What?

Pauline You're the fucking limit. Come on. We'd better get up reception and get you booked in proper.

Lauren Well, there might be a bit of a problem there . . .

Jackie . . . I knew . . .

Lauren . . . all I've got's a tenner, Tone lent me.

Jackie A tenner! A week-end away on a tenner?

Lauren No, it's got to last me all week.

Pauline and Jackie exchange a look, then Jackie scrambles for her bed.

Pauline (*throwing herself down on hers*) She's not having mine!

Lauren It's alright, I'll sleep on the floor. Won't be the first time. Here, this is gonna be menkle, innit? (*Toasts Pauline.*) Happy birthday, Pauline.

Pauline It's tomorrow.

Lauren I know. Funny innit, I forget everyone's birthdays, even me kids, but I always remember yours and Jac's.

Pauline God, we've had some fuckin birthdays over the years . . .

Lauren . . . This is going to be the best! More booze!

Lauren gets the vodka. Jackie gets her purse. Lauren offers her a cup of vodka.

Jackie No, ta. I got to call Rob.

Pauline (*laughs*) He can't smell your breath down the phone, Jac.

Jackie I just want to get it out the way. Then I can relax.

Lauren Thank fuck I don't have to check in whenever I go out. It's like being on license . . . Right then, what am I going to wear . . . ?

As Lauren starts to go through the pile of clothes on the bed –

Pauline (*to Jackie*) Shall I come with you?

Jackie God, why does everyone think I need me hand held all the time?

Pauline (*a bit taken aback*) I just thought you didn't want to go out on your own, wearing that . . .

Jackie stops. She'd forgotten about the clothes. But she has to make the call by herself.

Pauline . . . tell you what, we'll go to reception, and while you're on the phone, I'll go and do some shopping . . . (*with a marked look at Lauren*) . . . more vodka.

Lauren (*calls after Pauline and Jackie as they exit*) Cheers Paul – and twenty Silk Cut King Size.

Pauline turns, and sticks a finger up at Lauren, before exiting. Lauren laughs. She slops some more vodka in her cup, then spots Jackie's bag on the bed. She turns up the tape recorder. Opening bars of 'Devil-Gate Drive', by Suzi Quatro blasts out, as Lauren sits down on the bed, and starts to go through Jackie's bag.

Lights down. During the scene change 'Devil-Gate Drive' changes into 'Rockefeller Skank'.

SCENE TWO

Lights up on Boys' Chalet.

It's exactly the same as the girls' chalet – two beds, table, two chairs – only a lot tidier. No clothes on the bed, no clutter on the wash-basin. The duvet covers are a bit posher and there's a crate of Special Brew on the floor. 'Rockefeller Skank' is playing on Carl's portable CD player, which is on the table. Also on the table there's a pair of Dr Martens, standing on a sheet of newspaper. Vince is spraying the boots silver. Fade down music as –

Carl leaps into the room, from the hallway, brandishing his guitar. He's practising his big entrance – a Bolanesque flight across the stage.

Vince . . . they're my fucking kids, too. She can't tell me I can't talk to them . . . can she?

Carl How far was that, do you reckon? Ten foot?

Vince How'd she fucking like it if I did that to her – she can't pull strokes like that.

Carl How big's the stage, do you reckon? Twenty feet? Thirty?

Vince . . . she's got a problem. Innit, Carl? That woman's got a real fucking problem.

Carl You're her fucking problem.

He exits again, as Vince is saying:

Vince Yeah, too fucking right, I am, and this is one fucking problem she can't control. That's about the size of it. Innit Carl? I won't lie down and let her fucking walk all over me.

Carl makes his entrance again, not so far this time.

Carl (*about his entrance*) Crap. (*to Vince*) She still on about the money?

Vince Is she still on about the fucking money!

Carl Call me old-fashioned, but she needs a smack. Tell her to fuck off, Vince, she can't stop you seeing your kids.

Vince She has stopped me seeing the fucking kids. Now she won't even let them come to the phone – says they're watching the fucking telly and they don't want to speak to me. Bitch.

Carl shrugs and leaves the room again.

Vince She wants me to fucking pay her to see me own fucking kids. That's sick, innit? That's kidnap. And blackmail. (*Beat.*) She wants me to give up on them. But I en't gonna do it . . .

Carl flies across the room, punching the air, and saying –

Carl Rock on!

Vince What the fuck are you doing?

Carl Practising me entrance – 'He flies across the stage to the screams of his adoring fans, there isn't a dry seat in the house . . . '

Vince You what?

Carl I don't know what to say, that's the trouble – I thought 'rock on' like that old David Essex watsit, you think it sounds stupid?

Vince Don't matter what I think – you won't be doing none of it.

Carl Why not?

Vince You come on like that tomorrow night, and you're out on your arse, you daft cunt – there's only gonna be one of us making any fucking 'entrance', and it ain't gonna be the hired help. You hear what I'm saying?

Carl So what do *we* do?

Vince We play our fucking guitars, and we sing our fucking backing vocals. And we smile.

Carl Wah – fuck that – I've worked out me routine.

Vince Listen, I've done this gig before. Pwllheli, Easter. We had this blond kiddy, bit of a metal-head, he'd worked out a fucking routine and all . . .

Carl . . . mine's better than a spastic metal-freak . . .

Vince . . . he done it in the sound – check. That night 'someone' spikes his drink with acid, and the poor cunt's lying on the floor, backstage – he's sinking into blackcurrant jelly, and it's biting him . . .

Carl (*appreciative*) . . . good one . . .

Vince . . . next day he's home with his mum, and we're doing the tour with a grand-dad from Porthcawl. Get it now?

Carl Play. Sing. Smile.

Vince It's fucking ruthless – rock'n'roll.

Carl S'pose 'someone' gets first dabs at the minge and all?

Vince Don't you worry about the fanny. There'll be more than you can handle.

Carl Speak for yourself – I'm in me prime, me . . .

Vince That's another fucking thing she said – s'pose you'll be screwing slags all weekend, then . . . ?

Carl Too fucking right, you lucky bastard . . .

Vince . . . like, what the fuck's it to her who I knob now anyway – fucking women – they don't want it, but they can't let go of it . . .

Carl . . . my girlfriend's not like that. My girlfriend understands life on the road.

Vince Yeah, yeah – they all say that . . .

Carl . . . straight up – she knows. If she wants me, she's got to put up with my appetites.

Vince What – she don't mind you fuckin' around?

Carl I'm not saying she don't mind – 'course she minds – she just knows what I'm like. In-fuckin-satiable. I can't help it, it's just me, what I'm like. I'd get bored with the same cunt all the time, you know what I mean? You know – it gets too safe . . .

Vince (*laughs*) . . . dozy fucker.

Carl What?

Vince You wait. I don't care what she says now, what she lets you get away with now – she's putting the fucking screws on you. She's got your number.

Carl Bollocks.

Vince Just fucking watch out she don't get pregnant. They love that one . . .

Carl . . . look, I'm not fucking stupid – she's on the pill . . .

Vince laughs.

What?

Vince Where have I heard that before? 'It's alright darling, I'm on the pill.' Nah. Don't let me tell you. You'll see.

Carl gives him a look, crosses the room for a can of Special Brew.

Carl Want one?

Vince Yeah, go on then, me throat's as dry as fuck with this paint, innit? (*about the boots*) What do you reckon?

Carl (*chucking over a can*) Yeah. Look alright.

Vince Don't put them on yet – they're not dry.

Carl You what?

Vince I said, don't put them on yet . . .

Carl (*coming over*) . . . are those my fucking boots?

Vince Yeah. Thought I'd give 'em a bit of the old Bowies.

Carl Oy, you cunt – that's me fucking decent boots, that is, I don't want them all fucked with that glitter crap . . .

Vince . . . oh, pardon me for being helpful . . .

Carl (*trying to rub the paint off with newspapers*) . . . Jesus fucking Christ . . . ruined . . .

Vince . . . fuck off, they look great. You want to look the part, don't you?

Carl What fucking part? You told me I just got to fucking smile . . .

Vince . . . nah, that's tomorrow you just got to smile – tonight you're a fucking sex-machine.

Carl I don't need a poxy pair of silver boots to be a sex-machine.

Vince (*laughs*) Nah. Well, that ain't all you got to wear.

Carl What?

   Vince laughs again.

Carl Nah, fuck off. You're a wind-up. No wonder no other bastard wanted to share with you.

Vince That ent right, is it?

Carl Yeah. We fucking spoofed for you. I lost.

Vince Cunt.

Carl They were right and all.

Vince What?

Carl They said you'd go on about your ex all the time.

Vince Fuck off, I don't.

Carl You do, you're fucking obsessed – when did you split up, two years ago?

Vince Two years and three months . . .

Carl . . . yeah, exactly, most blokes would've forgot all about the cow by now.

Vince She's got me fucking kids, I can't just forget about her . . .

Carl . . . find someone else. Have some more kids.

Vince looks at him. Carl laughs.

Vince Fuck off.

Carl Tell you what, mate. Life's too fucking short.

Vince No, it ain't. It's too fucking long.

Carl You miserable bastard.

Vince You wait. I was like you ten years ago. All I wanted was mindless sex with as many dirty bitches as I could get my dick into – no names, no numbers – just fucking . . . you think that's any way to live your life?

Carl I don't know.

Vince Well. Let me tell you –

He stares at Carl, then laughs.

– it could be a lot fucking worse –

He sprays a bit of silver paint at Carl.

Carl Oy –

Lights down on the chalet and we are straight into a cover version of 'Sex-Machine' by James Brown (the cover is being performed by the Sensational Soul Boys, i.e. the band Vince and Carl are playing in tonight.)

The Mirage Bar.
Jackie, Pauline and Lauren are dancing by a table covered in plastic glasses. They are dancing to the funky sounds of The Sensational Soul-Boys, who are just reaching the end of their set. Pauline and Jackie are doing 'The Bump' together and Lauren is dancing by herself, self-aware. Pauline and Jackie are wearing the same as before: Jackie's left off the wig, and Pauline's wearing a pair of platform-boots she looks unsteady on. Lauren's wearing the green halter-neck and a pair of hot-pants and boots. With her hair done and make-up, she knows she's attracting a lot of looks and she loves it. As the song ends, the girls clap, shout, whistle, over –

Vince (*off*) Thank you, Minehead! – good night . . .

The girls continue to cheer in the hope of an encore, but almost immediately we go into 'Living Next Door to Alice' by Smokie with Roy 'Chubby' Brown. The girls pick up their nearly empty glasses from the table. Their conversation has to be pitched over the music.

Jackie Bloody hell, I haven't danced so much in years!

Pauline You want to get out a bit more.

Jackie nods emphatically, then adds:

Jackie Yeh, but where do you go that plays this?

Pauline Some places have 70s nights . . .

Lauren They're fucking crap. Full of kids.

Pauline Everywhere's full of kids.

Lauren You're supposed to stop enjoying yourself when you get to our age.

Jackie I'm all right then. I stopped enjoying myself years ago!

Lauren and Pauline laugh.

Lauren We ought to take her down The Mandrake.

Jackie In town?

Lauren Yeh, it's full of old slappers and little boys. You're guaranteed to score.

Jackie (*pulls a face*) No, thanks.

Lauren It's right, though, innit, Paul?

Pauline Yeh, if you just want to get groped by some spotty adolescent who's just discovered what his prick's for . . .

Lauren Yes, please! (*She drains her glass.*) Whose turn to go to the bar?

Pauline Can't be yours. You haven't been once yet.

Jackie laughs.

Lauren (*unperturbed*) We shouldn't have to buy our own drinks, anyway – we've been here fucking hours. Where's the men?

Jackie (*sings*)
'It's raining men – Hallelujah – it's raining men . . . '

Lauren (*over*) I'd have been all right if I'd been here on me own. I'd be fucking drowning in drinks.

Pauline (*holding out her glass*) All right, then. Mrs. Irresistible. Try your fatal charm on the bar staff.

Lauren Can't. I'm waiting for the guy in the band.

Pauline What guy in the band?

Lauren The little guy on lead guitar – didn't you see he kept smiling at me?

Pauline He was smiling at everyone.

Lauren (*chants*) You're just jealous 'cos I pulled first.

Pauline God – I didn't know it was a contest!

Lauren (*smirks*) No contest, my babs.

Pauline Well, some of us believe in quality over quantity.

Lauren Well, some of us can't get a shag.

Jackie What are you two on about?

Pauline Sex-on-legs here thinks she's pulled.

Lauren I have – I always do. I'm lush.

Pauline shoves her fingers down her throat and makes a gagging sound.

Jackie How'd you manage it, Laur? I wouldn't have a clue, it's been so long . . .

Lauren . . . it's still the same. Men are a piece of piss. Watch . . .

Lauren has a look around. She catches the eye of someone in the audience. She stares at him, then looks away. Then she looks back, really staring hard and smiling to herself. Pauline and Jackie are watching the guy.

Pauline Think you're being too subtle, Laur . . .

Lauren You wait.

A moment, then Lauren's grin broadens and the other two laugh. The guy is looking back.

(*Turning away*) Two-nil.

Pauline Are we supposed to be impressed? (*to Jackie*) Same again ?

Jackie Can I have a short this time? I'm getting bloated . . .

Pauline Vodka?

Jackie Lovely.

Lauren I'll have a brandy and Bailey's.

Pauline You'll have what you're given.

Pauline exits.

Lauren Is she pissy with me, or what?

Jackie (*shrugs*) I don't know. Maybe you shouldn't have told her she can't get a shag . . .

Lauren I was joking. 'Course she can get a shag, she just mustn't mind what's on the other end of it.

They both laugh.

Let's get her fixed up. I'll do it.

Jackie She doesn't want a one-night stand. She wants marriage and babies . . .

Lauren . . . bloody hell, leaving it a bit late, in't she?

Jackie She hasn't had a lot of choice.

Lauren It's crap. Marriage – kids . . .

Jackie It isn't.

Lauren You don't count, Jac, you've been married all your life.

The music subtly changes from Smokie to 'Kung Fu Fighting' by Carl Douglas.

Jackie So I don't got an opinion, right?

Lauren (*distracted*) Sshhsh – dance – pretend you haven't noticed . . .

Jackie Noticed what?

Vince and Carl come on from the other side of the stage. They are both dressed as soul-boys – afro-wigs, white flared trousers, red shirts open to the navel and black grease-paint on any visible flesh. Vince is wearing platform shoes, Carl is wearing his silver DMs. They start to dance to the record, making kung-fu moves on each other.

Oh, my god! It's really them.

Lauren Don't look. He's got to come to me . . .

They dance, seemingly self-absorbed, but with one eye on the lads.

Carl (*to Vince*) We might've got fucking changed first.

Vince And have no fucker recognise us? What's the point of being a star if you don't get your bit of adulation at the end of the day?

Carl I'd be a lot happier about my bit of adulation if I wasn't done out like Barry fucking White – why the fuck didn't anyone tell me we got to wear this shit?

Vince 'Cos of your fucking face when you realised.

Carl Cunts.

Vince What's your problem? It's only a fucking job, innit?

Carl I'm a fucking muso, not a black and white min-strel – we should've fucked off to a hotel with the other guys.

Vince I'm not spending the night in the residents' bar with Micky and Roger – fucking Roger – 'I used to be a Rubette, you know' – wanker. Anyway, what's up with you? I thought you wanted a pop at the crack.

Carl Yeh, after a shower or summat . . .

Vince Fucking strike while the iron's hot, I reckon, mate, while they're all still glowing from our fantastic set – see, that couple of old slags over there can't keep their eyes off us . . .

Carl Aren't we gonna have a look about a bit, first?

Vince Bit old, you reckon?

Carl Don't bother me, a few stretch-marks. Makes 'em keener to please.

Vince Never made my missis keener to please.

Carl Well, you're the cunt put them there in the first place.

Vince (*aiming a kung-fu kick at Carl*) Fuck off –

Carl spins round, kicks back at Vince, as –

Lauren Why isn't he coming over?

Jackie He's playing with his pal.

Lauren Fuck that for a game of soldiers. Come on . . .

Lauren links arms with Jackie and drags her over to the lads.

Jackie Lauren . . . !

Lauren (*to Carl*) Hiya.

Vince and Carl look at the girls.

Carl Hi . . .

Lauren You can stop playing hard to get.

Carl What?

Lauren You can have me if you want me.

Jackie Lauren!

Carl (*grins*) I know. (*to Jackie*) Who are you?

Lauren I'm Lauren and she's Jackie.

Carl Hi, Jackie.

Jackie Hello.

Vince Jackie. My sister used to read that.

Jackie So did I.

Vince Shut up, you're not old enough.

> *At this point, Pauline returns from the bar. She is trying to carry three shorts and not fall off her platforms.*
> *Jackie and Lauren fail to notice her unsteady progress. She sees them, though, and hesitates – wondering what to do.*
> *After being ignored for a moment, Pauline continues to the table, puts down the three glasses. She starts drinking, nose out of joint. The action is simultaneous with:*

Lauren She's the same age as me. Where're you from? You're not from round here, are you?

Vince (*American accent*) We're from the Land of Funk – the Country of Soul . . .

Lauren We're from Chipping Sodbury.

> *Vince and Carl laugh.*

Jackie It *is* a real place.

Vince (*West Country accent*) Oooh-arrr. Bet you loves a rollock in the hay with they mangel-wurzels.

Lauren I've seen The Wurzels.

Jackie So've I.

Vince I'm impressed! Aren't we, Carl?

Jackie (*laughing*) Shut up – I didn't mean it like that.

Vince So what brings you out of Chipping Sodbury, then? You're allowed to say me.

Lauren Me.

Jackie It's our friend's birthday –

Remembering Pauline, she looks around and sees her at the table. Pauline finishes her own drink and starts on Lauren's, studiously ignoring the others.

– oh. Laur –?

Jackie nods towards Pauline.

Lauren Oh, great – Pauline's back with the drinks. Go and get her, Jac.

As Jackie goes over to Pauline –

Lauren (*to Vince and Carl*) It's our mate's birthday, tomorrow. That's why we're here. Got a fag?

Vince shakes his head. Carl starts to extract a packet from his trouser pocket, as:

Jackie (*to Pauline, excitedly*) Paul – come and meet the band . . .

Pauline Oh, you remembered me, then?

She finishes off Lauren's drink and starts on Jackie's as –

Jackie Don't be daft – come on – they're nice . . .

Pauline We came here to see The Rollers. Not the bloody Robertson's Jam-Jars . . .

Carl is giving Lauren a cigarette. He lights it for her.

Lauren Cheers.

Jackie Don't be like that, Paul. Come on, before Lauren scares them off . . .

They both look over.

Lauren Got any drugs?

Carl Yes, thanks.

Jackie (*taking Pauline's arm*) And they might know where the Rollers are staying . . .

Pauline allows herself to be led over, holding a drink.

Lauren Only you can get drugs off the Red-Coats. I seen it in *News of the World* . . . all right, Paul? (*to Vince and Carl*) This is our mate, Pauline. She's going to be forty tomorrow.

Jackie Lauren!

Vince (*to Pauline*) The big four-oh, eh?

Pauline Summat like that – (*toasting Lauren*) – Cheers, Laur.

Lauren Is that mine?

Pauline It was – (*She knocks the drink back.*)

Lauren Pauline!

Vince Serves you right – you should never reveal a lady's age.

Pauline smiles at him. She has now had three shorts in quick succession and is feeling very amiable.

Pauline She's a mouthy bag, isn't she? . . . I thought you were very good.

Lauren (*to Vince*) You're in there.

Jackie Oh yeh, you were brilliant! Sounded just like the records . . .

Vince (*smiles at her*) Thanks.

Carl So are we going to get a fucking drink then, or what?

Lauren Yeh, are we going to get a fucking drink then, or what?

Vince gets a ten pound note out of his pocket, hands it to Carl.

Vince There you go. Get yourself a bag of crisps while you're up there.

Carl (*not taking the note*) It's not the money – I'm not queuing at the bar like a fucking punter . . .

Lauren (*taking the note*) . . . I'll go.

Vince Oy –

Carl (*laughs*) What is it with you and women and money?

Lauren (*linking Carl's arm*) You come with me and keep me company.

Carl Insistent bitch, aren't you?

Lauren I never take no for an answer.

Pauline Never gives no for answer, either.

Vince laughs. Pauline grins at him.

Jackie (*a bit affronted*) I'll come with you, Laur.

Lauren I can manage . . . .

Carl I can't.

Vince (*to Jackie*) You're not leaving me, are you?

Jackie I don't want to be in the way . . .

Vince (*quietly*) You're not, Jackie. You're not.

The others haven't heard this. Jackie looks embarrassed, but pleased.

Lauren Right then – drinks for everyone – except for Pauline, for being a greedy bitch . . .

Vince Doubles for Pauline, for her birthday . . .

Lauren Ooh – watch out, Paul – he's trying to get you pissed . . .

Lauren exits with Carl, Pauline smirks at Vince.

Pauline She's so embarrassing. Can't take her anywhere.

Vince Why'd you bring her then?

Pauline Oh god. Do you really want to know?

Vince Try me.

He smiles at Jackie.

Pauline Well, we've been best friends since school. Us three. Well, me and Jac, really, innit, Jac?

Jackie (*smiles at Vince*) Yeh.

Pauline Lauren's just – well – around. Anyway, when we were at school we were mad about the Rollers . . .

Vince . . . no taste . . .

Jackie (*protests*) Oy –

Vince Were you a Rollerette?

Jackie Oh, yeh – I had all the tartan . . .

Pauline . . . we seen them at the Colston Hall – didn't we, Jac? Best night of my life, ever. I snogged Woody.

Vince laughs.

Jackie She did.

Vince (*still amused*) No, I believe you . . .

Jackie They was magic. First time I'd ever felt so excited about summat – and all those other girls, excited, just set me off worse . . .

Pauline . . . we was all waiting outside, pushing – it was really hot, wasn't it? – and when they came out, they just got in their van, we couldn't see them . . .

Jackie . . . but they couldn't drive off, there was too many girls in the way . . .

Pauline . . . I'll never forget it. I opened the door. I don't know what made me. I just had to.

Jackie I couldn't believe it. She was mad . . .

Pauline . . . and I just went 'Woody', and he put his arms round me – still makes me go funny to think about it . . .

Vince (*laughing*) Did you do tongues?

Pauline I don't care if you don't believe me . . .

Vince No, I do. So that's why you're here, then – The Rollers.

Pauline Never saw them again. I thought it'd be a crack for me birthday – summat different . . .

Vince It'll be different all right.

Jackie Have you ever met them?

Vince Yeh.

Jackie Have you? What are they like?

Vince Bunch of tossers. Sorry, but they are. 'Cept for Woody. He's all right.

Pauline Do you know Woody?

Vince Oh yeh. We're like that, me and Woody.

Pauline I don't believe you . . .

Vince I don't care if you don't believe me . . .

Pauline . . . oh, I didn't mean it like . . .

Jackie (*over*) I do.

Vince Do you? Why?

Jackie I don't know. I just do . . .

Pauline . . . no, I wasn't saying I *don't*, really . . .

Lauren and Carl are coming back, Carl's carrying a tray of drinks, and Lauren is waving one of those fluorescent wand things around.

Lauren . . . look what I got! Fucking lush, innit?

Carl (*to Pauline and Jackie*) What's she on?

Pauline Yeh, well, we got all weekend with her . . . (*to Vince*) . . . thanks for the drink . . .

Vince ignores her, he's moved in on Jackie.

Vince That means summat to me. You believe me.

Jackie Well, why would you lie? You're in a band, you'd know famous people . . .

Vince . . . and now I know you.

Jackie I'm not famous.

Vince You stand out in this crowd.

Vince takes a drink from the tray and gives it to Jackie. She smiles up at him. They stare at each other as Pauline looks on, disappointed.

Lauren (*waving her wand*) I'm going to magic us the best night ever . . . .

The music goes into 'Seasons in the Sun' by Terry Jacks.
Lights down.

The Girls' Chalet.
 *The room is empty – lit by an orangey light on the
wall outside. Off, in the next chalet, we hear a couple
arguing loudly but incoherently – he is shouting, she is
screaming back. Then glass smashing. There's a silence,
broken by Jackie, Lauren, Vince and Carl returning from
the bar. Jackie, Lauren and Vince are singing:*

Jackie/Lauren/Vince 'We had joy, we had fun – we
flicked bogies at the sun – '

 They are now at the door, trying to unlock it.

'But the sun was too hot so the bogies turned to snot . . .'

 *As they all come into the room, the music stops. Vince
is practically carrying Jackie. He sits her down on the
bed, she immediately falls back, closing her eyes.
Vince sits next to her, stroking her leg. Lauren turns
on the light, then heads for the cider bottle. Carl starts
to go through the tapes.*

Lauren (*singing with the bottle*) 'I am the cider-drinker.
I drinks it all of the day . . . (*opening bottle*) . . . ooh ar,
ooh ar ay – ooh ar, ooh ar ay . . . '

 *Lauren sloshes cider down her throat, before holding
out the bottle to Carl. There is a hammering on the
wall.*

Carl (*to wall*) Fuck off.

 He drinks the cider, spits it out.

Jesus! What is it? Tastes like cow's piss . . .

Jackie (*still comatose*) Where's Pauline?

Lauren (*to Jackie*) She's all right, Jac . . . (*to Carl*) It's only scrumpy . . .

Carl No wonder you lot shag sheep . . .

Lauren Don't knock it till you've tried it.

Vince Woody fucks goats.

Jackie Is she here?

Vince Woody's goat?

Lauren (*to Jackie*) Pauline's all right, Jac – don't worry . . .

Jackie . . . it's her birthday . . .

Carl (*to Lauren*) Where is she?

Lauren Having a lie down on the crazy golf.

Carl laughs and turns on the music – 'Pillow Talk' by Sylvia. He gets hold of Lauren and they start to dance together. Vince lies down with Jackie.

Jackie Where's Pauline?

Vince Pauline's all right. Pauline's great . . .

Jackie . . . it's her birthday . . .

Vince . . . yeh, I know – shhsh . . .

Vince puts his arms round Jackie, tries to kiss her. She moves her head away.

Jackie Don't.

Vince Talk to me then . . .

Carl and Lauren are really getting into their smooch – Lauren is rubbing herself against him.

Jackie I'm tired . . .

Vince Don't go to sleep. Talk to me . . . (*He strokes her leg.*) . . . do you like that?

Jackie No.

Vince You do . . .

He moves his hand further up her leg, then kisses her. After a moment, Jackie pulls away, laughing.

Jackie No!

Vince Yes . . .

He tries to kiss her again, Jackie tries to sit up. After a brief struggle, Jackie succeeds.

Jackie I need a drink.

Vince (*sitting up*) Stay there, I'll get it. Cider?

Jackie Vodka.

Vince picks up the vodka bottle from the sink. It's empty.

Lauren (*over Carl's shoulder*) Pauline drank it.

Vince (*to Jackie*) You're out of luck . . .

Jackie There's a bottle of champagne in my bag . . . under the bed? I got it for Paul's birthday . . .

Vince That's all right – we'll get her another one.

Vince looks in Jackie's overnight bag for the champagne. Carl and Lauren are still dancing.

Jackie Serves her right, anyhow. Going off like that. (*Sees herself in the mirror.*) God, I look a mess . . .

Vince has got the (not very expensive) champagne. He leans over the bed and kisses Jackie's cheek.

Vince . . . you look fucking gorgeous . . .

Jackie You're just saying that.

Vince I never say anything I don't mean.

He kisses her other cheek.

I love you.

Jackie (*laughs*) Stop it!

Vince I mean it.

He straightens, opens the champagne, saying:

We'll get her a much better bottle than this. I wouldn't clean my teeth in this.

Jackie Well, yeh – rock star. You'll be wanting to throw the telly out the window next.

Vince (*amused*) Are you getting smart with me?

He holds the foaming bottle out to her.

Jackie Not *getting* smart – I *am* smart . . .

Jackie takes a swig and chokes.

Vince (*laughs*) That'll teach you . . .

Jackie mock-punches him, still coughing. Lauren doesn't turn her head, or falter in the dance, but stretches out a hand.

Lauren Whang that over here . . .

Vince takes the bottle from Jackie and puts it into Lauren's hand. Lauren takes a swig, then pulls Carl's mouth onto her own, feeding him champagne. They kiss passionately, still moving to the song. Vince stares down at Jackie, now recovered.

Jackie What?

Vince Kiss me.

Jackie No.

Vince Dance with me.

Jackie No.

Vince Come on . . .

He pulls her up. They dance together.

Carl (*to Lauren*) Do you take it up the arse?

Lauren Do you?

Carl laughs and hugs her.

Carl You're great . . .

They kiss again.

Vince (*to Jackie*) Don't be nervous.

Jackie I'm not.

Vince I know you want me . . .

Jackie laughs.

Vince . . . you are beautiful, really, really beautiful . . .

He tries to kiss her again.

Jackie . . . Vince . . .

Vince I can't help it. You're driving me mad. I love you . . .

Jackie . . . you don't know me . . .

Carl (*to Lauren*) Have you got a shower in here?

Vince . . . I feel like I've known you all my life . . .

He stops dancing and holds Jackie's face in his hands. Stares down at her as –

Lauren Why?

Carl Will you piss on me?

Lauren laughs.

Jackie (*to Vince – a bit shakily*) I bet you say that to all the girls.

Vince No. I don't.

Carl No one's ever done that for me.

Lauren Really?

Jackie Yeh, but – there's nothing about me . . .

Vince You can't see it, can you? But I can . . .

Jackie stares up at him.

Carl (*to Lauren*) You'd be the first.

Lauren looks at him.

Lauren All right then.

Carl leads Lauren from the room. Lauren is still holding the bottle of champagne.

Jackie Where are you going, Laur?

Carl She's just giving me the guided tour.

They are out of the room. Jackie sits back down on the bed.

Jackie She would take the bloody champagne.

Vince stands over her.

Vince How many kids have you got?

Jackie Two. How did you know?

Vince touches the lines on her eyes.

Vince These.

Jackie covers the lines with her fingers.

Jackie Don't.

Vince (*taking her fingers away*) Don't be stupid.

They look at each other.

So who's got them tonight then – their dad?

Jackie Yes.

Vince He's lucky. My ex won't let me have mine overnight.

Jackie Why not?

Vince Yeh, my point, exactly. Why not? She's just a fucking cow, Jackie. She uses them to get at me.

Jackie Oh, that's not fair . . .

Vince . . . it's not, is it? They need me and I need them. She won't see it, she wants to be everything . . .

Jackie . . . yeh, but they need their dad as well.

Vince That's right.

He sits down next to her.

Fucking right.

Jackie How many children have you got?

Vince Two.

Jackie Boys or girls or . . . ?

Vince Boy and girl. One of each.

Jackie Me, too! What are your's called?

Vince Let's not talk about them now, all right?

Jackie (*shakes her head*) . . . no – all right . . .

Vince . . . I don't want to think about them right now . . .

Jackie . . . no, I'm sorry, 'course not . . .

Vince strokes her face.

Vince Lovely . . . lovely mum . . .

Jackie Vince –

Vince . . . sshsh . . . let me . . .

He leans over and kisses her. This time Jackie kisses him back. A moment, then we hear – off the sound of a shower spattering onto a cracked tile floor, simultaneous with a shriek from Lauren.

Lauren (*off*) It's fucking freezing!

Her shrieks don't disturb Vince and Jackie, who lie back on the bed, snogging passionately. Music – 'Could It Be Forever' by David Cassidy. Lights down on chalet.

SCENE FIVE

The crazy golf-course. Pauline is sprawled out on Hole Nine with a half-bottle of vodka. She is talking to a garden gnome, fishing from a bridge.

Pauline (*sings*) . . . are the stars out tonight? I don't know if it's cloudy or bright – 'cos I only have eyes for you . . . (*She drinks, laughs.*) . . . hello? . . . talk to me . . . (*She waits.*) . . . don't then . . . (*She drinks.*) . . . you won't catch anything, you know – there's no fucking water . . . (*She laughs, chokes, sits up, laughs.*) . . . shot to bits, birthday girl . . . I'm cold . . . (*to gnome*) . . . lend us your hat . . . bastard. It's me birthday . . . (*She drinks.*) . . . happy birthday, forty fucking . . . fuck-life.

Didn't even get a birthday kiss – big surprise, stupid bitch, who wants to kiss you? (*to gnome*) You don't – do you? . . . (*Waits.*) Why? What's the matter with me? (*Drinks.*) Why don't you want me best? It's all I want. It's all I fucking want – I don't want to be alone, I don't want this, it's not fair, I don't want this, I want to be wanted . . . I want Woody. I want Woody. I want Woody. I want Woody. I want Woody . . .

Woody appears in the shadows. He is wearing all his Bay City Rollers gear – white trousers with the tartan strip, a short-sleeved white jumper with red trim on the sleeves and neck and a red W on the front. Pauline looks at him. She smiles.

All right? I've missed you. You look bloody great . . .

Woody stands there. Pauline smiles at him. Gradual lights down. Music – 'Give a Little Love' by the Bay City Rollers.

SCENE SIX

The Girls' Chalet.
    It's early Saturday morning – about 6 am. Vince and Jackie are asleep in Jackie's bed. Carl and Lauren are asleep in Pauline's bed. Everyone's clothes are all over the floor. As the lights go up, we hear knocking on the chalet door. It's a bit tentative at first, but then it gets louder. The music goes out.

Pauline (*off*) Jackie! *Jackie!*

There is no reaction from the sleepers. Pauline knocks harder.

Jackie! It's me – Pauline! Let me in!

44

Inside the chalet, Vince stirs. Throughout the next section of dialogue, Vince opens his eyes, realises where he is, and very, very quietly, gets out of bed. He is naked, with a smudgy triangle of black dye on his chest (where it would show beneath the costume) and on his face. Pauline is still knocking.

Jackie! Please . . . it's freezing . . .

Male Voice (*off*) . . . *Fucking shut up!* There's people trying to sleep here . . .

Pauline (*off*) . . . I'm locked out! I can't get in . . .

Vince is tiptoeing over to wake Carl.

Male Voice (*off*) . . . I couldn't give a fuck. Shut the fuck up!

Vince prods Carl, who wakes with a snort.

Carl What – ?

Vince shakes his head, warningly, finger to his lips. Carl starts to sneak out of bed. He is naked, too.

Pauline (*off*) Well, thanks a bunch.

Vince and Carl are getting dressed – pulling on clothes as they find them. Pauline knocks on the door again, though not so loudly.

Male Voice (*off*) I'm warning you, you stupid cunt.

No more knocking. Carl holds up a sock.

Carl (*whispers*) This yours or mine?

Vince (*whispers*) It doesn't matter – let's just get.

He looks over at Jackie. She's still asleep, curled up on the side of the bed.

Carl (*whispers*) It fucking stinks in here.

Vince (*whispers*) Your bird spewed.

Carl looks over at Lauren. There is a small stream of sick trailing down the side of the bed and onto the floor. Lauren's head is in it.

Carl (*whispers*) Ugh, she's fucking lying in it.

Vince (*whispers*) Dirty bitch.

Carl (*whispers – proudly*) She's that all right.

Vince picks up his shoes.

Vince (*whispers*) Come on.

Carl (*whispers*) Hang on – I can't find me other shoe . . .

Vince sighs, and exits. While Carl is looking under the bed, we hear the chalet door being stealthily opened, off, then –

Vince (*off*) Morning . . .

Pauline (*off*) About fucking time.

Carl can't find his shoe under Lauren's bed, so looks under Jackie's. Pauline is coming through the door. She looks cold, tired and hanging. She is carrying her platform boots. Vince appears in the doorway, behind her.

Pauline (*surveying the scene*) Jesus.

Vince (*to Carl*) Come on!

Pauline (*loudly*) Wake up, Jac! Time for breakfast!

Jackie stirs.

Jackie What?

Vince (*to Carl*) Look in the bathroom.

Vince withdraws again.

Pauline (*to Jackie*) . . . time for your lovely fry-up . . .

Carl is exiting to the bathroom, Jackie is sitting up, confused.

Jackie Paul . . . ? (*Last night comes flooding back.*) Oh, god . . .

Vince reappears in the doorway, at the sound of Jackie's voice.

Vince (*to Jackie*) Hi.

Jackie (*looking away, disconcerted*) All right?

Pauline The boyfriend's busting for his breakfast, isn't he? Can't wait to get over there. (*to Vince*) What's yours – the full monty? Or are you more of a poached egg on a slice of wholemeal man?

Jackie (*queasy*) Don't, Paul . . .

Pauline (*noticing Lauren's sick*) . . . oh, for fuck's sake!

Jackie I'm sorry.

Then Jackie sees Pauline is looking at the sick.

Oh, god . . .

Pauline (*shaking Lauren*) Wake up – Lauren – come on – get up . . .

Jackie is avoiding looking at Vince. Carl appears behind Vince, in the doorway, now wearing his shoes.

Carl Got 'em.

Pauline Lauren!

Lauren rolls over, mumbling.

Vince Right then . . .

He looks at Jackie. She's huddled into herself, staring down at the bed.

. . . Jackie? . . .

Jackie doesn't look up. Pauline looks at her, looks at Vince.

Pauline Why don't you just go?

Vince What's it to you?

Pauline Just fuck off. All right? I've been locked out of my bed all night, thanks to you two wankers . . .

Jackie makes a little noise of apology, still not looking up at all.

Carl (*to Vince*) Are we done then?

Vince shrugs, looks at Jackie.

Vince Aren't you going to say goodbye?

Jackie won't look at him.

Jackie?

Jackie Goodbye.

Vince Thanks for a great night.

Carl Yeh – cheers . . .

A moment, then Vince turns away. Carl heads off in front of him. Jackie looks up, but Vince and Carl have gone. We hear the chalet door open and close. Jackie looks at Pauline. Pauline's been watching her all the time. They hold each other's look for a moment.

Vince (*off*) Ever fucked seaweed?

Carl laughs. A beat.

Pauline Come on – give me a hand with this . . .

48

Jackie Pauline – I'm so sorry . . .

Pauline Good.

Jackie You must really hate me.

Pauline I am freezing cold and exhausted – I hate everyone . . .

Jackie I don't blame you – honest, but I thought you were right behind us, Paul – what happened?

Pauline I don't know. I woke up on the archery range. Fucking worst night of my life.

Jackie gets out of bed, pulls on a teeshirt. She looks utterly miserable.

Jackie Have my bed.

Pauline looks at her, then gets into the bed. She pulls the cover up over her head. Jackie, meanwhile, pours herself a glass of water. She finds her bag and starts looking for her Paramol. They're not there.

Paul? Sorry to bother you – you haven't got any pain-killers have you?

Pauline grunts a negative.

. . . I could've sworn I had some . . .

She sips the water. Stares at the two beds, and the two motionless forms. Moment.

Paul? What am I going to do?

Pauline (*under cover*) Do about what?

Jackie You know! Oh, please don't be mad at me – I don't know what happened, I don't know why I did it . . .

Pauline pushes back her cover.

Pauline . . . you were pissed.

Jackie I know, but it's no excuse, is it? Oh god. I wish I was dead!

Pauline It wasn't that bad, was it?

Jackie You don't understand – I feel awful. Really, really horrible. I am the most horrible person in the world . . .

Pauline . . . oh, don't make such a thing of it! At least you weren't abandoned by your bloody mates on your bloody birthday and left to freeze to death in the middle of bloody Butlins – anything could have happened! I might have got gang-banged by a mob of bloody Red-Coats!

Jackie They wouldn't do that.

Pauline They wouldn't bloody do it to *me*! At least you got a shag, Jac!

Jackie I didn't want it!

Pauline Raped you, did he?

Jackie doesn't say anything.

Look, it's happened – all right? Forget it.

Jackie How can I forget it? I'll never, ever be able to forgive myself – one night away from home and I end up like this. Oh god. What about Rob? How can I face him after this?

Pauline He's not going to know, is he?

Jackie I'm going to know. It's always going to be there, between us – you don't know what it's like, Paul, he's my husband, he trusts me – oh, I wish I'd never come here . . .

Pauline gets out of bed.

Pauline Right. Well, let's go straight home then, shall we?

Pauline pulls the covers off Lauren, who is sleeping in just the halter-neck.

Pauline Get up, Lauren, we got to go . . .

Jackie . . . hang on, I didn't say that . . .

Lauren (*waking*) . . . what's happening?

Pauline We're leaving. Get up.

Jackie I never said we had to go . . .

Lauren I got sick in me hair . . .

Pauline . . . you said you wished you'd never come. Let's go then.

Jackie No.

Lauren . . . the fucking bastard spewed in me hair!

Pauline (*to Jackie*) Why not? (*to Lauren*) It's your sick, Laur.

Lauren Oh. (*getting out of bed*) That's all right, then.

Lauren pulls on a pair of knickers.

Jackie I don't want to go yet.

Pauline Hoping to see your lovely boyfriend again, are you?

Jackie No! I hate him – I wish I'd never laid eyes on him . . .

Pauline That's not all you laid on him, is it?

Lauren laughs. She pours herself a glass of water, during –

Jackie Paul, please – if you understood how awful I feel, you wouldn't say that . . . .

Lauren Got a headache, Jac?

Jackie Yes.

Lauren (*fishing in her hot-pants*) I got your pain-killers in here, somewhere . . .

Jackie How? They were in my bag . . .

Lauren . . . yeh, I took them out – they're all right with alcohol . . .

Jackie What the hell were you doing in my bag?

Lauren Just having a look. You don't mind, do you?

Jackie Yes, I do! How would you like it if I went through your bag?

Lauren I wouldn't care. We're mates, aren't we? We don't have any secrets . . .

Pauline You two don't. Not after last night . . .

Lauren laughs – throws a pack of Paramol to Jackie.

Lauren . . . yeh – just like old times, wasn't it, Jac?

Jackie No . . .

Lauren . . . yeh, you know, those couple of bikers we used to cop off with – me and AJS Ashley and you and old whatsisface . . .

Jackie I don't remember . . .

Lauren You do. We used to go down Ashley's garage and take it in turns on the mattress . . .

Jackie . . . shut up, Laur .

Pauline I never heard about this.

Lauren Well, you wouldn't have, Jac always said not to tell you, 'cos you were still a virgin and she had to pretend she was too . . .

Jackie . . . that's not true!

Lauren Yes it is – you used to say Pauline would be jealous . . .

Jackie I don't remember any of this! Honest, Paul . . .

Pauline I don't care! Whatever you and Lauren got up to is nothing to do with me. Glad you had such a good time together – taking it in turns for the mattress – very romantic . . . .

She gets her bag out from under the bed and starts to pack.

Jackie What are you doing?

Pauline What's it look like?

Jackie I told you – I don't want to go . . .

Pauline . . . you don't have to. You and Laur can stay here and re-live all your yesterdays. I'm getting out the fucking way.

Jackie But it's your birthday, Paul – that's why we're here, we can't go back just because . . . we're only here for you . . .

Pauline . . . it's no skin off my nose. I fucking hate it here.

Lauren I think it's great.

Jackie (*to Pauline*) You're not going.

Pauline I want to. I'm tired and I'm fed up and I'm forty – it's just as bad as I thought it would be . . .

Jackie . . . Paul, I know, and it's all my fault, you've had a really shit night, and I'm sorry . . .

Pauline . . . it's not just your fault, it's hers and all . . .

Lauren . . . hey, I haven't done nothing . . .

Pauline . . . yeh, nothing by your standards . . .

Lauren . . . oh, don't start having a pop 'cos you lucked out on a fuck.

Pauline . . . lucked out? *Lucked out?* You've got to be fucking joking haven't you, they were pigs – arrogant, selfish, big-heads . . .

Lauren . . . so why'd you spend all night trying to tap off with them, then?

Pauline *I didn't . . .* !

Jackie . . . stop it – stop it – *stop it*!

In the sudden silence that follows, there is a hammering on the next-door wall. The three women burst into slightly hysterical laughter.

Pauline (*to wall*) Get a life.

Lauren (*to wall*) Wanker.

Pauline (*to Jackie*) Your go.

Jackie Oh, I can't think of nothing – I don't know . . . (*to wall*) . . . arseholes!

Lauren Oh god, that reminds me . . .

Pauline What?

Lauren Nothing – look, we're not really going to go home, are we? We haven't seen the Rollers, yet . . .

Jackie . . . yeh, we can't go back without seeing the Rollers, Paul, that's the whole point . . .

Lauren has been rummaging about in her carrier-bag, and produces a book.

Lauren Happy birthday.

Lauren gives Pauline a Bay City Rollers Annual – it's an old one she found in a charity shop.

Pauline (*touched*) Oh – what?

Lauren Good – innit?

Pauline It's brilliant! Cheers, Laur . . .

Pauline makes a move to kiss Lauren, then changes her mind.

. . . ugh, get in the bloody shower . . .

Jackie . . . I got you champagne . . .

Pauline's looking at her book.

Pauline . . . oh, look – Les . . . Derek – you fancy Derek, don't you, Laur?

Lauren Ugh – naus.

Jackie . . . she drank it . . .

Pauline Ah, there he is. My Woody. (*She kisses the page.*)

Lauren Bet he don't look like that now.

Pauline Who cares? He'll always be my Woody – I'm not one of these fair-weather fans who only likes you if you're in the charts. He might be a sad old has-been washed up in Butlins in the middle of November, but he'll always be my baby . . .

Jackie . . . Pauline, you can't leave! I know you think we let you down, but last night wasn't really your birthday, was it? Today's your birthday, and tonight it's the Rollers . . .

Lauren (*sings*) 'Tonight's the night – everything's all right . . . '

Jackie You can't go without seeing Woody . . .

Beat.

Pauline Woody's my boyfriend . . .

Jackie . . . I go out with Les . . .

Pauline . . . we talk all the time. He says I'm the only one who really understands him. He says we're going to be together for ever . . .

Jackie . . . Les and I are going to get married . . .

Lauren What are you on about?

Jackie and Pauline look at each other and smile.

Pauline I'm going to look after him. In our house. By the sea. Woody and me . . .

Jackie . . . and we'll come and stay – me and Les and the kids . . .

They both laugh.

Pauline (*punching the air*)
B-A-Y! B-A-Y!

Jackie joins in.

Pauline/Jackie (*together*)
B-A-Y, C-I-T-Y –

Lauren joins in.

Pauline/Jackie/Lauren (*together*)
With a R-O-double-L-E-R-S,
BAY CITY ROLLERS ARE THE BEST!

As the lights go down, we hear frantic hammering on the wall.

Male Voice (*off*) You've got it coming!

End of Act One.

Act Two

We are still in Butlins. Not caught the train home, yet.

Aqua-Splash – the Sub-Tropical Water World.
In one part, Vince is sitting on a white plastic chair by the pool-side, wearing swimming-shorts and reading a paper. Sun-glasses on his head. There's another chair next to him, with a towel over it, and a pair of sun-glasses on the chair. Two cans of beer by the chairs.
In another part, Pauline and Lauren are lying out on towels. Lauren's smoking a cigarette and checking out the life-guards. Pauline's reading a magazine. There's a bag next to them, with an opened bottle of white wine concealed inside.
We can hear the shouts and screams of excited swimmers in the pool.

Lauren Now – there's nobody looking . . .

Pauline surreptitiously gets the bottle from the bag, and passes it to Lauren. At the same time, Carl is coming on. He's just got out of the pool, and he's wet. As he nears Vince, he shakes himself – like a dog – all over Vince and his paper.

Vince (*lowers paper*) Oy!

Pauline Careful, Laur – the life-guard's looking . . .

Lauren puts the bottle behind her.

Lauren He fancies me.

Pauline gives her a look, and buries herself in her magazine. Lauren smiles langorously. Carl is vigorously drying himself with his towel.

Carl Come on, you ponce, get in the water – it's great. Sort out your hangover.

Vince I have not got a fucking hangover.

Carl Yeh, right. You should see your fucking eyes, man. They're yellow . . .

Vince looks at Carl, then pulls his sunglasses down over his eyes, turns back to his paper. Carl finishes getting dry and sits down on the chair. He picks up his can. Meanwhile, on the towels:

Lauren Shall I go swimming and pretend to drown?

Pauline What for?

Lauren So he can give me the kiss of life.

Pauline You live in a dream-world, don't you?

Carl opens his can, offers it to Vince. Vince shakes his head. Carl drinks.

Lauren Me? What about you and Jac and that Les and Woody crap?

Pauline Didn't you ever have a fantasy boyfriend?

Lauren No. I was too busy with the real ones.

She gets the wine out again, and drinks. Pauline turns a page in her magazine.

Carl Did you see me on the chute?

Vince No.

Carl I came down backwards – you should've been watching . . .

Vince lowers his paper.

Vince Are you me fucking kid? 'Can you see me, Dad?'

Carl Great for kids, pool like this. D'ya ever take your kids to Butlins?

Vince Nah. Nah, they'd have loved this. She doesn't think of that, does she? Why couldn't they come here with me?

Carl (*sarcastic*) That would've been fun . . .

Vince Selfish cunt.

Carl Me?

Lauren (*reflectively*) I brought me kids here once . . .

Pauline gives her a little sidelong glance, but doesn't say anything.

Vince . . . nah, Mrs. 'I'm so knackered, I've got such a headache, I'm a single parent . . . ' she bangs on about needing a life, but *I* can't have the kids for a weekend, can I? Might make me start to look good and we can't have that . . .

Lauren has another swig of wine.

Carl Did you ask her?

Vince What's the point? You get fed up with the knock-back – you know, you think of something that'd be nice to do, you're planning it in your head, and then she goes, 'No'. I don't fucking bother any more.

He goes back to his paper. Carl swigs his beer.

Lauren Nah, come to think of it – it wasn't here. It was Barry Island. And I didn't take them – Alan did.

Pauline looks at her.

Pauline Can't you remember what you did with your kids?

Lauren Yeh . . . summat . . . gets a bit blurry . . .

Pauline Might help if you didn't drink so much.

Lauren I might not *want* to remember . . .

Vince Bitch.

Carl Who?

Vince Fucking Sue – I didn't do anything – she just went all moody on us – you know, 'Why've you got to be out all the time? – I'm fed up sitting here on me own every night with two kids screaming at me . . . '

Carl I wouldn't fucking have that, mate . . .

Vince . . . I didn't get it – she knew what I did, I'm not a fucking nine-to-five wanker. I thought she liked it. But suddenly, it's all wrong – she can't cope, it's too much doing it all on her own, and I can't help her, won't let me try – she'd rather fuck me off and be mother-fucking do-it-all saint single-parent smug-hypocritical cow . . .

Carl Right.

He sips his beer.

Gonna try the sun-beds?

Vince (*back in his paper*) No.

Lauren Pauline?

Pauline Huh?

Lauren You did want me to come, didn't you? Only you sort of looked a bit pissed off when I showed up . . .

Pauline Shut up – of course I wanted you here. You're

me best mates, you and Jac, you've been me best mates since school . . .

Lauren Yeh, well, you know. Two's company – three's a crowd.

Pauline Why'd you say that?

Lauren Well, it's always you and Jac, and me tagging along . . .

Pauline It isn't! What about last night – it was you and Jac, wasn't it? I was the one bloody tagging along last night . . .

Lauren . . . reminded me when we all used to go out, and I'd always get asked to dance first – then Jac might get a dance, and you'd be really pissed off with us . . .

Pauline Lauren!

Lauren What?

Pauline Rub it in.

Lauren I'm only saying . . . best days of me life they were . . .

Pauline . . . what – better than getting married and having your kids?

Lauren Work it out . . .

Vince You know what it really is? With Sue? It's got fuck-all to do with me being away – she won't fucking say what it really is, but I know . . .

Lauren . . . why am I not with my husband and my kids?

Vince She thinks I'm a failure. She doesn't want her kids brought up by a failure, you know, I'm not fucking Elton, am I? I'm just a sad cunt doing covers in a holiday-camp . . .

Pauline Sometimes I just don't get you, Laur.

Lauren (*happy*) I know.

She swigs her wine. Pauline stares ahead, lost in thought.

Carl Your missis don't think that . . .

Vince . . . she fucking does – what she doesn't know is it's all down to the breaks, luck – I can play any fucking thing those other cunts can – I can write songs – only they got the chances, and I didn't . . . I could've done summat that was me, summat fucking original . . .

Carl . . . yeh, well, what the fuck's original? Y'know? Everyone's copying now – you take someone like Oasis, or the Spices, they got to record, they got to tour, they got to do drugs and practise their dance routines – so how can they be there for everyone who wants them there? Tribute bands, mate. The world fucking needs us.

Vince gives a dismissive snort.

I'll tell you something else – people go and see these bands? – they're not thinking – this isn't as good as the real thing, most of the time it's better, 'cos we're better fucking musos, and we're there for the crack, we're not all 'fuck the audience, we're the stars', we're up for it and they're loving it . . .

Vince (*laughs*) . . . yeh – wish you could say all that to my missis . . .

Carl Fuck her. There's plenty of tarts that do appreciate it – what about your bird last night?

Vince Yeh – she was fucking well chuffed about the band, wasn't she?

Carl There you go . . .

Vince . . . she was nice . . .

Lauren Are we getting back to Jac, now?

Pauline doesn't reply.

Paul . . . ?

Pauline What?

Lauren You're miles away. Thinking about Woody?

Pauline I was just thinking – I wish I'd had your life. You had it all. I wouldn't fuck that up.

Lauren Fuck it up?

Pauline You know – you never see your kids . . .

Lauren (*sniggers*) Good . . .

Pauline Lauren – don't be so fucking cruel . . .

Lauren (*getting up*) Well, it's none of your business.

Pauline Sorry.

Lauren You wish you'd had my life? Dream on. Nobody but me gets my life . . .

She starts to exit. Pauline follows.

Carl Oh, fuck.

Vince What?

Pauline Lauren – I'm sorry. What I meant come out wrong . . .

Carl It's those tarts from last night – don't look –

Carl slips his sun-glasses on.

They might not recognise us without the wigs – *don't look –*

He pushes Vince's paper up over Vince's face

(*Turning right round to Vince*) Here, you know who I saw once? The Son of Elvis . . .

Pauline . . . I'm forty, Laur, all that matters to me . . .

Carl . . . I mean, that's what he called himself – there wasn't any proof . . .

Vince lowers his paper and watches as Pauline and Lauren pass – they don't look at Carl and Vince at all – meanwhile, Carl is still telling his story, his whole body turned away from the girls.

Carl . . . he didn't look like Elvis, didn't even sing like him . . .

Pauline . . . why can't you just admit it matters to you?

Lauren stops. Pauline stops, and waits.

Carl . . . he came on stage saying he was Elvis's son, and the minge went mental. I thought I might do that when I've finished this one. Say I'm the son of Gary Glitter or summat . . . (*He laughs.*)

Lauren I couldn't give a flying fuck.

Vince watches as Lauren turns away and walks off in the opposite direction. After a moment, Pauline exits too.

Carl Poor old Gazza . . . his fucking tribute band's fucked . . .

Vince It wasn't her.

Carl Who?

Vince Jackie.

Carl Oh – right. It was mine, though, wasn't it? I'd know those nipples anywhere . . .

Vince Hope she's all right.

Carl . . . chapel fucking hat-pegs.

Vince Shouldn't have just fucked off like that this morning.

Carl Shut up.

Vince She *was* nice.

Carl (*laughs*) You sound like a schoolboy . . .

Vince . . . that's just it, I'm not a fucking schoolboy – one night stands, bollocks – you meet a nice lady and you fuck her off. Crap. (*Moment.*) She's got kids. She knows what it's like . . .

Carl looks at Vince. As the lights fade on Carl and Vince, Noddy Holder yells 'Baby, Baby, Baby' and we are into 'Cum on Feel the Noize' by Slade.

SCENE TWO

The Public Telephone.
It's on a wall, in a row of telephones. Slade are blaring out of a loudspeaker, as Jackie tries to have a conversation with Rob. She has one finger jammed in her ear. She is out of her glam-gear and wearing 90s winter casual.

Jackie . . . I'm sorry, Rob, I can't really get them to turn it down, there's no one on reception . . . yeh, I know, it seems a weird choice of music – perhaps they think it'll cheer everyone up after all the aerobics and the bread and water . . . (*She laughs, a bit nervously.*) . . . no, not really, it's quite nice, really – grilled chicken, steamed veggies, did you have the lasagne last night? . . . was it all right – what? . . . oh, um, nothing really . . . well, no, we went for a run this morning, and I've just got back from a swim . . . yeh, I know that's 'something', so what about you? Going out today? . . . yeh, I know it's hard with the kids, I didn't mean you *had* to go out . . . I wasn't . . . I wasn't having a go, Rob . . . do I? I don't mean to sound funny . . . yes, of course I miss you, you know I'm only here for Pauline . . . well, it's not my fault it's women only – some places are like that . . .

Jackie turns, still holding the phone. Vince steps from the shadows. She sees him looking at her, turns away and speaks quickly:

. . . I've got to go . . . to the gym . . . no, I can't, they get funny if you're late – I'll call you later . . . yeh, 'bye . . . I love you . . .

Jackie puts the phone down. She moves away, she is shaking, she feels so nervous. She looks over at Vince. He walks towards her. He, too, is wearing 90s clothes, suitable for mid-November.

Vince Phoning your kids?

Jackie Yeh.

Vince Are they all right?

Jackie Yeh.

There's a moment, he's looking at her. She looks away.

Jackie I'd better be getting on . . .

She starts to walk off –

Vince You do remember me, don't you?

Jackie (*stops*) Yes.

Vince Thought you mightn't . . . without the wig . . .

Jackie (*smiles slightly*) . . . it wasn't just the wig, was it?

Vince grins.

66

Vince No . . . look – this morning – it was crap, I'm sorry . . .

Jackie That's all right.

She tries to walk past him again. Vince touches her arm.

Vince Do you fancy a ride on a rickshaw?

Jackie Eh?

Vince Take in the sights – the car parks, the chippy . . .

Jackie . . . I thought you'd be gone by now.

Vince Nah, we're . . . (*Stops himself.*) . . . no rush.

Beat.

Jackie I don't think so.

Vince Look. This morning I behaved like a cunt. Sorry. But I did. I don't know why – you're so nice and . . . special.

Jackie I ought to get back to the others.

Vince Why?

Jackie 'Cos I ought. Last night was . . . (*She shrugs.*) . . . it wasn't me – I don't do that sort of thing . . .

Vince I know. You're special.

Jackie No – you mustn't say that.

Vince Jackie – look, I know you're not a slag. Last night meant something to you, and it did to me, too. This morning . . . I didn't know what to say. I'm just not used to feeling this way . . .

Jackie looks at him, doesn't say anything. Vince laughs.

I'm a poet and I didn't know it. Make a good line for a song that, wouldn't it? 'I didn't know what to say, guess I'm not used to feeling this way . . . ' (*Beat.*) I'll call the song 'Jackie'.

Jackie You're going to write a song about me?

Vince Yeh.

Jackie laughs, pleased.

Jackie Well, remember me when you get to number one.

Vince Yeh, I will. I'll never forget you.

They look at each other. Beat.

Jackie I used to write songs. Well – poems, really, but I'd make up the tunes, too . . .

Vince Sing me summat.

Jackie I can't – this is years ago . . . gave up all that when I had the kids.

Vince That's a shame.

Jackie I wasn't going to do anything about it. I'm not that sort of person . . .

Vince . . . bollocks. You go for it. You only got one life, haven't you?

Jackie It's a bit late – I'm forty next month.

Vince Life begins at . . .

Jackie (*laughs*) Don't say it!

Vince Maybe your life began when you met me.

Jackie You mustn't say that, either.

Vince Why not?

Jackie Because I can't – and you can't – you don't really mean it . . .

Vince Yes, I do.

Jackie But you don't *know* me . . .

Vince So? I'm an incurable romantic. (*Laughs.*) I am, you know, I really am – I thought she'd cured me, destroyed all that, but she hasn't . . . she can't. I feel great!

Jackie (*nervous laugh*) Great.

Vince Let's get married.

Jackie Don't be daft.

Vince Well, come for a drink, then – not here, we'll go into town, I've got the car . . .

Jackie I can't, you know I can't, I'm with me mates. It's Pauline's birthday.

Vince She won't mind. She wants you to enjoy yourself.

Jackie (*laughs*) She bloody well *will* mind! Look, she's been planning this for ages, our Rollers reunion . . .

Vince I'll tell you what. You come with me now for a drink, and I'll get Woody to sing to your mate.

Jackie You can't do that.

Vince 'Course I can. He'll do it tonight – on stage, in front of everyone – he'll sing 'Happy Birthday'. She'd like that, wouldn't she?

Jackie Not too much!

Vince It's done then.

Jackie And can she get to meet him, after?

Vince Well, I don't know about that . . .

Jackie Oh, go on. Please. You don't know what it'd mean to her . . .

Vince . . . s'pose you want to meet him and all?

Jackie No. I'm not interested in Woody.

Vince (*moving in on her*) Good . . .

Jackie (*ducking away*) I love Les.

Vince grabs her, picks her up. Jackie shrieks.

Jackie No – no – you'll drop me . . .

Vince is whirling her round.

Vince . . . take that back . . .

Jackie . . . put me down! . . . I'm too heavy! . . .

Vince . . . take it back . . .

Jackie . . . Vince! . . . no! .. please . . .

Vince Come on . . .

Jackie . . . I take it back . . . I take it back . . .

Vince lets her slide back down. They're still hanging on to each other. Lights down on Vince and Jackie as they kiss – and into 'Shang-a-Lang' by the Bay City Rollers.

SCENE THREE

Girls' Chalet / Boys' Chalet simultaneously.
  As the lights come up on the chalet, and the Bay City Rollers continue to sing, we can see Pauline and Carl getting changed. They are in what appears to be the same room, but completely unaware of each other, because, of course, it isn't the same room. 'Shang-a-

*Lang' is playing on Pauline's cassette recorder on the
sink and on Carl's sound system on the table. They are
both getting changed into Bay City Rollers' outfits –
Pauline is putting on a pair of jeans with the tartan trim
and a denim jacket trimmed with tartan; Carl is just
wearing a white wide-collared shirt and tartan waistcoat.
They move around each other, picking stuff up off the
bed, looking in the mirror, checking the window. They
are both anxious, waiting – and it's getting late. Carl
drinks a glass of whisky, Pauline is back on the vodka.*

Carl (*singing along*) . . . 'and we sang Shang-a-Lang,
and we ran with the gang, singing Shoo-wop-dee dooby-
do ay . . . '

*He picks up his guitar and mimes playing and doing
Rollers-type kicks to the next bit:*

'. . . we were all in the news, with our blue-suede shoes,
and our dancing the night away' . . .

*His mobile-phone rings. He puts down the guitar and
turns off the song. It carries on playing on Pauline's
cassette-recorder. Carl answers the phone.*

Hello? . . . oh, hi, darling (*Puts a finger in his ear.*) . . .
yeh, I know it's fucking noisy, the walls are thin and the
punters are thick . . . what? . . . well, I do feel fucking
stressed, sweetheart, Vince has fucked off, I don't know
where – didn't show for the soundcheck . . . yeh, going
fucking apeshit – wanker – it's not my fucking fault . . .
what's that? . . . yeh, 'course I'm a good boy, you know
I am . . . yeh, you better be and all . . . yeh, I love you . . .
yeh, more than that . . . keep it warm for me . . .

*Carl turns the phone off, throws it down on the bed.
He starts to put on a pair of tartan trousers. Pauline
has finished dressing. She turns off the music. She sits
down on the bed. She picks up her book, looks at it,*

then puts it back down. She is trying not to cry. A moment. We hear a door opening, off. Jackie comes into the chalet, she is looking happy and excited.

Jackie Pauline, guess what . . . ?

Pauline You were abducted by aliens.

Jackie What? Oh, right – look, I'm sorry, I was longer than I thought I'd be – but, Paul . . .

Pauline . . . where've you been? Only when I left you here this morning, you said you couldn't go out. And when I get back? You're gone.

Jackie Yeh, I know – the thing is, I went to phone Rob, and then I saw Vince again . . .

Vince is coming through the door – but only Carl reacts to him.

Pauline . . . oh, for fuck's sake . . .

Carl . . . oh, for fuck's sake . . .

Vince Don't be like that.

Jackie Oh, Pauline don't be like that. He's a nice guy, he really is. You'll never guess what he's going to do.

Carl You missed the fucking sound-check.

Pauline I don't want to know . . .

Vince I know.

Jackie But, Paul, it's brilliant, and it's a surprise for you.

Pauline looks at her. Vince starts to get undressed. Jackie looks at her watch.

Oh shit. I'd better get changed.

Jackie starts to get undressed. Carl grabs up a pile of clothes from the bed, and throws them at Vince.

Carl You haven't got time. You'll have to get changed over there – come on, we got to fucking go . . .

Vince picks up some things that have fallen on the floor.

Pauline Well, aren't you going to tell me what your boyfriend's going to do for me?

Jackie I told you! It's a surprise.

Carl Aren't you going to tell me where you've been?

Vince You're not my mum, are you?

Jackie Anyway, he's *not* my boyfriend, I can't have a boyfriend – you know that.

Pauline What is he then?

Jackie looks at her. Carl looks at Vince.

Carl You dirty bastard.

Vince smiles and shrugs, as he and Carl start to leave the room.

Jackie I don't know. Paul. I don't know what's happening to me.

Vince switches off the light, as he and Carl exit. The girls are plunged into darkness.

Pauline Fuck – the meter . . .

Pauline scrabbles around for a pound coin, as Jackie continues.

Jackie I've never felt like this before, he makes me feel special and wanted . . .

Pauline . . . and what about Rob? He makes you feel special and wanted.

Jackie . . . he doesn't, not like this – you don't know, Paul, I can't explain . . .

Pauline . . . don't explain. I don't want to hear!

Pauline puts a coin into the meter and the light comes back on. Jackie continues to get changed.

Pauline I'm pissed off – you know how much I was looking forward to this weekend, I thought we'd have a great time, the two of us . . .

Jackie . . . three of us . . .

Pauline . . . is this what it's all about? 'Cos I invited Lauren as well?

Jackie What all what's about?

Pauline The crap time I'm having! This is my worst birthday ever, and I've had some shitty birthdays in my time – my eighteenth, when I drank that guy's cider by mistake and he dropped the nut on me, my twenty -first, when I didn't go out, didn't do anything . . .

Jackie . . . Pauline, this isn't about *you* . . .

Pauline . . . is that supposed to make me feel better . . . ?

Jackie . . . I didn't expect this, I didn't mean for any of this to happen, but it has, and I know it's crazy and useless . . .

Pauline . . . does he know you're married?

Jackie No.

Pauline You told him you're single?

Jackie I didn't tell him anything, he just assumed.

Pauline So what are you going to do? Run away with this guy?

Jackie No! How can I? There's nothing I can do – I hate it . . .

Pauline No – I fucking hate it – I want that, you know, want a perfect stranger to fall in love with me and whisk me off somewhere, out of my life, and you know what? I thought it was going to happen this weekend – I thought it has to happen, I deserve it, it's my birthday . . .

Jackie . . . Pauline, it might . . .

Pauline . . . it bloody has. Only you got it, not me –

Looking up to the heavens.

– you cross-eyed or summat, God?

Lauren, off, bangs on the chalet door – and keeps banging till the door is answered. Jackie jumps.

Jackie Oh, God.

Pauline No, Lauren. But God knows what state she's in, she's been out all day. She got the hump 'cos I tried to talk about her kids . . .

Jackie . . . oh, Paul – you shouldn't – you know she doesn't like to . . .

Pauline . . . yeh, go on, stick up for her . . .

Jackie . . . I'm not . . .

Pauline Really fucking bonded this weekend haven't you? – just like the old days when you used to go trapping off together and leave me out . . .

Jackie . . . oh, shut up, Pauline, that's got nothing to do with it . . .

Over this, outside, we hear –

Man's Voice (*off*) I fucking warned you!

Jackie and Pauline react as we hear the sound of a man dropping the nut on Lauren. Lauren drops to the ground.

Jackie (*hurrying to the door*) Oh my god!

Pauline's going after her – we hear the chalet-door open, off.

(*Off*) Lauren! . . . oh, god – Lauren! What happened?

Pauline (*calls, off*) You bastard! I hope you're bloody proud of yourself, you stupid mental fuckwit . . .

Jackie (*off*) . . . Pauline, shut up – he might come back – we got to get her inside, christ, she's bleeding everywhere . . .

Pauline (*off*) . . . I can't touch her, Jac, I can't . . .

Jackie (*off*) . . . don't be stupid, you've got to help –

Lauren, off, makes a horrible groaning noise.

I can't pick her up by myself, and we can't just leave her here . . . please, Paul . . .

A beat, then we hear the unmistakable sound of two drunk women lifting a semi-conscious drunker woman off the steps of a chalet in Butlins and bringing her inside. Jackie and Pauline come through into the bedroom, Lauren between them. She looks a mess, she is bleeding from a broken nose. Pauline is trying not to heave.

Jackie Get her on the bed, Paul . . .

Jackie and Pauline lay Lauren down on Pauline's bed. She groans again. Pauline moves away, making a little retching sound. Jackie's going to the sink to get water.

Are you all right?

Pauline Yeh – you know what I'm like about blood.

Jackie Yeh, I do. Cheers, Paul, you're a mate . . .

Pauline looks at Lauren, quickly looks away again. Jackie's cleaning Lauren's wound.

Pauline Shall I go up reception? Get them to call an ambulance?

Jackie Yeh – no. Hang on. We can't do that. She's not supposed to be here, is she?

Pauline Yes, but we can't just . . .

Jackie . . . we'll all get into trouble if they find out. They might call the police.

Pauline So they fucking should call the police – look what's happened to her . . .

Jackie . . . Paul, I can't – if Rob finds out he'll kill me . . . look, she's not that bad . . .

Pauline . . . if Rob finds out about what?

Jackie I'm not supposed to be here either . . .

Lauren (*sitting up*) . . . I'm gonna be sick . . .

Jackie (*helping her*) . . . not in here, Laur – the bathroom . . .

Pauline .. what do you mean? I don't get it, Jac – why aren't you supposed to be here . . . ?

Jackie is helping Lauren out of the door into the bathroom.

Lauren . . . my head hurts . . .

Jackie . . . you're all right, Laur, you're going to be all right.

They exit. Pauline sits down on the bed. Off, retching from the bathroom. Jackie comes back in.

Have we got a cloth or summat?

Pauline Just tell me what's going on?

Jackie I told Rob we were going to a health-farm. Women only –

Pauline snorts incredulously.

– he wouldn't have let me come *here* . And I really
wanted to come, Paul, I didn't want to let you down . . .

Pauline . . . why wouldn't he let you come?

Jackie He doesn't want me to do anything – he doesn't
trust me – and it isn't worth the rows, Paul – it really
isn't . . .

Pauline You should have told me.

Jackie I was going to – before we got back . . .

Pauline . . . no, before – you always cracked on you had
the perfect bloody marriage . . .

Jackie . . . no – you said I did, 'cos you wanted it – you
never listen and I'm fed up with everyone having a go –
you're my wife, Jac, you've got to do this – you're my
mate, Jac, you've got to do that – I'm pissed off trying to
please everyone . . .

Lauren (*off*) . . . Jac!

Pauline . . . you're mental. I wouldn't let *anyone* tell me
I can't go where I want . . .

Jackie (*going back to the bathroom*) Don't give me that.
You haven't got a clue . . .

*More retching from the bathroom. Pauline notices
blood on her hands and clothes. She washes her hands
in the sink, tries to get the blood off her trousers.
Jackie comes back in. Pauline looks at her.*

Pauline That's why you didn't want to go home this
morning, isn't it? 'Cos you couldn't explain that to Rob.
It had nothing to do with my birthday or the Rollers . . .

Jackie . . . oh my god – the Rollers! (*Checks her watch.*)
Paul, they've started – you've got to go!

Pauline Forget it . . .

Jackie . . . no, you have to – Paul, it's really, really important – please, Pauline, *please* . . .

Pauline . . . I don't want to, any more.

Jackie Look – I know this weekend has been a total bloody disaster, but I promise you – if you go to the Rollers now, everything is going to be all right . . .

Pauline looks at her.

. . . it's that thing, Paul, that thing I told you Vince was going to do . . .

Pauline . . . what is it?

Jackie (*shakes her head*) I'm not going to tell you, you have to go – go on – *now* . . .

Pauline . . . but what about . . . ? (*She gestures to the bathroom.*)

Jackie She's all right, more arseholed than anything – I'll keep an eye on her. Go on, Pauline. You've got to go. Go for all of us . . .

We hear, over, the sound of clapping and cheering, and the B-A-Y – C-I-T-Y – R-O-L-L-E-R-S chant from a hundred throats. Lights down on the chalet. Clapping and chanting into the next scene –

SCENE FOUR

The Mirage Bar.
  Clapping, cheering and chanting. Lights up on Pauline. She is trying to see, she's right at the back of the crowded bar.

Les McKeown (*off*) Thank you – thank you – you've been terrific . . .

Pauline tries jumping up and down – she still can't see a thing.

– but before we go tonight, my friend, Woody here has got a special message for a young lady called Pauline – is there a Pauline Smith here?

Pauline stops jumping. She looks stunned. She puts up her hand.

Pauline (*small voice*) Me. I'm Pauline.

Les McKeown (*off*) Has anyone seen Pauline? Pauline the Birthday Girl . . .

Pauline (*shouts*) It's me! Woody! It's Pauline . . . !

A spotlight swivels and catches her. Pauline screams.

Pauline Woody!!

The band play a chord – Pauline is standing open-mouthed, transfixed with delight.

Vince (*sings off*) 'Happy Birthday to you .. Happy Birthday to you . . . Happy Birthday, dear – Pauline – (and I'll never forget the great snog we had) . . . Happy Birthday to you . . . '

Throughout the song, Pauline continues to stare, but by line three she has realised, and she starts to shake her head.

Pauline (*to herself*) Woody . . . .

At the end of the song, there is more clapping and cheering, but Pauline just stands there.

Lights down.

Girls' Chalet.
Lauren is lying on the bed, with a wad of damp toilet paper on her forehead. Jackie is bringing her a cup of tea.

Lauren Cheers. Has it stopped bleeding?

Jackie lifts the toilet paper and checks.

Jackie Not quite – be careful when you sit up . . .

Lauren gingerly sits up, holding the toilet paper in place.

Lauren What a cunt. I mean, what a fucking moron. He thought I was Pauline, didn't he?

Jackie I don't know . . .

Lauren She is really fucking for it, now. First she slags me off in the swimming pool, then I take a nut for her . . .

Jackie . . . oh, Lauren – shut up. She lugged you in here, didn't she, and you know what she's like about blood . . .

Lauren . . . yeh – god, do you remember Biology when we dissected that bull's eye? Down she went – hey, it's just as well she never had kids, she'd never have got through the birth . . .

Jackie It isn't too late . . .

Lauren It is, Jac – admit it – Pauline is never going to get a man.

Jackie That's tight.

Lauren It's true. You hang on to Rob, Jac – it's harder than you think out there.

Jackie But you do all right.

Lauren I don't want anything.

Beat.

Jackie Anyway. Pauline's meeting Woody right now – perhaps he'll be the man of her dreams after all, and she'll look back on this weekend as her best birthday ever . . .

Lauren Yeh, Pauline's got Woody and I got a bust nose, and you got – what did you get, Jac?

Jackie I don't know.

Moment.

You know when you met Barry . . . what was it like?

Lauren Biggest fucking mistake of me life.

Jackie No, but you didn't think that at the time, did you? – I mean, you gave up everything to be with him.

Lauren I didn't give up *anything* for Barry. Nothing that mattered.

Jackie But Lauren, you left Alan, you left your kids . . .

Lauren . . . yeh, left me sad little life for another sad little life, what a tosser. Still, we live and learn, don't we?

Jackie (*stares*) I don't get you . . .

Lauren No, you don't, and neither does Pauline, and I'll tell you what, I'm sick to death of the both of you waiting for me to crack, get off on a guilt-trip, 'cos I'm not fucking going to. Me kids are much better off without me around all the time, pissed up, going on at them, and I'm better off by meself without any fucker expecting anything of me. I got a great life . . .

Jackie . . . you haven't, Lauren, that's rubbish, you're just a drunk.

Lauren Drunk and happy. (*She laughs to herself.*) Drunk and happy . . . (*Exclaims.*) – fucking hell!

Vince is standing in the doorway, dressed as Woody out of the Bay City Rollers. Jackie turns.

Vince Sorry – the door was open . . .

Jackie . . . Vince?

Vince . . . where were you? I thought you were going to come up on stage – (*clocking Lauren*) – fuck, what happened to her?

Lauren I got mistook.

Jackie (*to Vince*) Why are you wearing those clothes?

Vince I'm Woody, aren't I? I told you we were like that . . . (*Holds up two fingers pressed tightly together.*)

Carl is coming into the room, still dressed as Derek.

Carl C'mon Vince, for fuck's sake, His Nibs is getting petulant . . .

Jackie . . . but you're not – you're not really Woody . . .

Vince Well, I'm not the Woody that plays in Fat Eric's Bay City Rollers, and I'm not the Woody that plays in The Rollers 90s Revival, but I am the Woody that plays in Les McKeown's Bay City Rollers . . .

Carl . . . yeh, and your master's waiting, Mr Wood . . .

Lauren (*to Carl*) . . . which one are you supposed to be?

Carl (*looks at her*) Jesus. What happened to you?

Jackie (*to Vince*) Oh my god. You didn't sing to Pauline, did you?

Vince Yeh, 'course I did. You told me to . . .

Lauren (*to Carl*) Come and kiss it better.

　Carl grimaces, Lauren laughs.

Vince (*to Jackie*) look, I've got to go, we've got a gig in Chesterfield tomorrow night, and the van's broken down, so I have to drive – rock'n'roll, eh?

Jackie She is going to go spare . . .

Vince Come with me.

Jackie I can't!

Lauren I can.

Carl You can't.

Vince Jackie – try – just another night – we can stay in a hotel.

Jackie . . . no, wait, I've got to get this sorted – where's Pauline?

Vince I don't know. She was there – I sang to her . . .

Jackie . . . I told her you had a surprise for her – she'll think I set it all up . . . (*to Vince*) . . . why didn't you tell me Woody was you?

Vince He's not. I'm him. Bit metaphysical, innit . . .

　Pauline is coming through the door.

Pauline Ha – ha.

Jackie Pauline. I didn't know . . .

Lauren . . . all right, Paul? Was it good?

Pauline (*to Lauren*) . . . yeh. Fucking creaser. Did you know and all?

Jackie . . . listen, Paul – I didn't . . .

Vince (*to Pauline*) What's your problem?

Pauline What?

Vince I said – what's your problem? Your mate arranged a surprise for you, and so what if it wasn't the Woody you wanted, I'm fucking Woody tonight.

Lauren (*laughs*) That should be fun!

Pauline (*turns*) Do you want some fun, Laur?

Carl Vince! We got to go . . .

Pauline (*over him*) . . . Jackie told Rob she was away at a health-farm. A women-only health farm!

Lauren laughs.

Talk about under the thumb.

Jackie Shut up, Pauline, don't tell her . . .

Pauline (*to Lauren*) Imagine what he said when I told him where she really was?

Jackie What!

Vince Who's Rob?

Pauline (*to Jackie*) You had your fun – I had mine . . .

Jackie You bitch! You rotten fucking bitch .

Jackie slaps Pauline.

Vince . . . hoy . . .

Pauline (*pushing Jackie*) . . . you're the fucking bitch round here!

Carl . . . aye, aye – handbags at dawn . . .

Pauline . . . have a fucking laugh with your new bloke – my stupid mate, Pauline, still believes in happy endings . . .

Jackie (*at the same time*) . . . I never done nothing to you. Nothing! He told us he knew Woody, I thought he really meant it, why do you think I'd be so tight . . . ?

Lauren . . . it's right, Paul – she didn't know – tho' I don't blame you for getting pissy . . .

Pauline stops, stares.

Jackie . . . so what do you say now? Eh? Now you've fucked up everything for me?

Pauline I haven't.

Jackie Yes, you have. You jealous bitch. You're made up now, aren't you?

Pauline Jealous? What – of you?

Jackie Yeh – me – I've always had what you haven't got, and you've always made sure I know it – 'Oh, when will I get a boyfriend? When will I have kids like you?' Like my life's fine because I got Rob, I'm not allowed to be unhappy, you're the one who's unhappy – you're no friend, Pauline. You're just a stupid selfish bitch I used to go to school with and we got nothing in common. Nothing!

Pauline turns and runs from the chalet. Everyone is staring at Jackie .

. . . I don't care! It's true!

Beat.

Vince Who's Rob?

Jackie My husband.

Vince Your ex.

Jackie No. My husband. We live together – we're married.

Vince (*nodding*) Right.

86

Carl Right then. Let's go.

Lauren I'm not married.

Vince You want to come then?

Jackie You can't take *her* . . .

Vince . . . I can't take *you*.

Lauren Yeh, all right, then. Brilliant.

She gets up and starts cramming her stuff into a carrier, still holding her 'bandage' in place.

Carl He's not going to like this . . .

Jackie Lauren – you can't go, you mustn't . . . (*to Vince*) . . . why are you doing this? I thought you liked me . . .

Vince . . . why didn't you tell me you got a fucking husband?

Jackie I don't know.

Vince Not very important?

Jackie hangs her head and mumbles.

Jackie I couldn't – you liked me . . . I didn't want to let you down . . .

Vince . . . let me down? What the fuck's that about?

Jackie I don't know – I just . . . do what people want, I'm used to . . . don't have a go at me. Please . . .

Vince . . . it was just a fuck . . .

Jackie . . . no . . .

Vince And you just say, 'No thanks, I'm married' or 'Yes please, I'm married'. Then we all know the fucking score.

Jackie is still staring at the floor.

Lauren I'm ready.

Jackie No! (*going to Vince*) Don't do this to me . . .

Vince . . . he's there looking after your fucking kids, isn't he? Poor bastard. I know what it's like.

Beat. Jackie turns away.

(*To Lauren*) Come on then.

Lauren (*to Jackie*) See you soon . . .

There is a move to the door.

Carl (*exiting*) . . . we're not really going to take her, are we . . . ?

Vince (*exiting*) . . . why not? Summat to do on the way . . .

Lauren (*exiting*) You wait. You're gonna fall in love with me.

We hear her laugh, then the chalet door closes. Jackie stares after them for a moment, then she hauls out her bag from under the bed, and starts to pack. Lights down on chalet.
Music – 'Bye, Bye, Baby' by the Bay City Rollers – sounding as if from far away.

SCENE SIX

The Crazy Golf Course.
It is late at night. Pauline is sitting by her friend, the fishing-gnome. Jackie comes on, carrying her bag.

Jackie I've been looking for you, everywhere.

Pauline doesn't say anything.

I'm going to get a cab back home.

Pauline It'll cost a fortune.

Jackie I want to go home.

Beat.

Pauline I didn't call Rob, by the way.

Jackie What?

Pauline I didn't call him – I never said I did. I said 'Imagine I told him'.

Jackie Is that true?

Pauline Yeh. I might be a fucking selfish bitch, but I'm not *that* much of a fucking selfish bitch . . .

Jackie . . . Pauline – I didn't mean it . . .

Pauline . . . yeh, you did. You're right. We've got nothing in common. Apart from being forty . . .

Jackie . . . no, Paul – we're friends . . .

Pauline . . . no, we're a habit. Like you and Rob's a habit. People in your life you feel you're stuck with . . .

Jackie Lauren's gone off with Vince and Carl.

Pauline Good. She'll really wind them up.

Jackie I couldn't have gone . . . the kids . . .

Pauline Know summat, Jac? I don't want your life. I've been thinking – this is me. By meself. Alone. So fucking what?

Jackie Pauline, you will meet someone . . .

Pauline How come? Is there a law that says everyone has to be in a couple, or a threesome, or a baker's fucking dozen? I might be meant to be this – might be my whole purpose in life to be me, not Mrs Someone, not the girlfriend. I might fucking need this.

Beat.

Jackie I'm going home.

Pauline Suit yourself. Tell Rob you got expelled for smuggling jammy-doughnuts. I'm stopping on for Suzi Quatro.

Jackie I'm going to tell him, Paul.

Pauline Why?

Jackie Because . . . I want to. (*She gives a short laugh.*) That's why.

Jackie leaves. A moment. Pauline puts out her hand.

Pauline Woody? Are you there?

There's a moment. Then 'Woody' appears, spotlit in the shadows – just as before. Pauline smiles.

It's over.

The light goes on 'Woody'. Music – 'Young Hearts Run Free' by Candi Staton.
   Lights fade on Pauline.
   The End.

Discover the brightest and best in fresh theatre writing with
Faber's new StageScripts

Sweetheart by Nick Grosso   0571 17967 3

Mules by Winsome Pinnock   0571 19022 7

The Wolves by Michael Punter   0571 19302 1

Gabriel by Moira Buffini   0571 19327 7

Skeleton by Tanika Gupta   0571 19339 0

The Cub by Stephanie McKnight   0571 19381 1

Fair Game by Rebecca Prichard   0571 19476 1
(a free adaptation of **Games in the Backyard** by Edna Mazya)

Crazyhorse by Parv Bancil   0571 19477 X

Sabina! by Chris Dolan   0571 19590 3

I Am Yours by Judith Thompson   0571 19612 8

Been So Long by Che Walker   0571 19650 0

Yard Gal by Rebecca Prichard   0571 1959 1

Sea Urchins by Sharman Macdonald   0571 19695 0

Twins by Maureen Lawrence   0571 20065 6

Real Classy Affair by Nick Grosso   0571 19592 X

Skinned by Abi Morgan   0571 20007 9

Down Red Lane by Kate Dean   0571 20070 2

Dogs Barking by Richard Zajdlic   0571 20006 0

All Faber *StageScripts* are priced at £4.50.
If you cannot find them stocked at your local bookshop
please contact Faber Sales Department on 0171 465 0045